FIREFIGHTING

VGM'S CAREER PORTRAITS

FIREFIGHTING

Blythe Camenson

 VGM Career Horizons
a division of NTC Publishing Group
Lincolnwood, Illinois USA

Photo Credits:
Pages 1, 15, 29, 43, 57, and 71: Photo Network, Tustin, CA.
All other photographs courtesy of the author.

Library of Congress Cataloging-in-Publication Data

Blythe, Camenson.
    Firefighting / Blythe Camenson.
       p.   cm. — (VGM's career portraits)
    Includes index.
    Summary: Presents information on the various duties of
  firefighters including emergency medical services, fire
  investigation and prevention, training, and administration.
ISBN 0-8442-4374-4 (hardback)
    1. Fire extinction—Vocational guidance—Juvenile literature.
  2. Fire fighters—Juvenile literature. [1. Fire extinction—
Vocational guidance. 2. Fire fighters. 3. Vocational guidance.]
I. Title. II. Series.
TH9119.C36 1995   95-18541
628.9'2'023—dc20   CIP
                                     AC

Published by VGM Career Horizons, a division of NTC Publishing Group
4255 West Touhy Avenue
Lincolnwood (Chicago), Illinois 60646-1975, U.S.A.

5 6 7 8 9 0 QB 9 8 7 6 5 4 3 2 1

Contents

Late last night, when we were all in bed
Old Lady Leary left a lantern in the shed.
When the cow kicked it over, she winked her eye
    and said,
"There'll be a hot time in the old town tonight."

Dedication

To all the brave men and women at the Boca Raton,
Deerfield Beach, and Pompano Beach Fire Departments
in South Florida.

Introduction

When most people head out for work in the morning, they have a pretty good idea what the day will have in store for them. In a firefighting career, each hour, even each minute, can bring something different, something unexpected. Firefighters *never* know what situations they'll encounter during the day.

Because most fire stations across the country function as combined fire and rescue departments, most firefighters are cross-trained. Their duties cover much more than battling blazes. Firefighters today are generally all EMTs, or emergency medical technicians. Many are paramedics. They respond to just about every emergency imaginable. They use the Jaws of Life to extricate victims trapped in cars; they climb tall buildings, or dive underwater. They deal with dangerous gases and other hazardous materials, investigate how fires started, and teach fire safety and prevention to schoolchildren and civic groups. They even rescue frightened animals stuck in drainpipes or wells.

Firefighters go through a rigorous training program. They must be physically fit and courageous enough to meet any challenge. Are you ready to meet the challenge? Then read on and see if firefighting is the right career for you.

FIREFIGHTERS

Do you get excited when you hear sirens and see all the colorful lights flashing? Do you love to watch the fire trucks whiz by and wish you could be going along for the ride?

Firefighters are a special breed. They are go-getters, team players, and strong-minded individuals who know how to get a job done and done well. Do you share those qualities? If so, then read on and learn about all the different jobs within the fire service.

1

What it's like being a firefighter

Because most fire departments combine fire with rescue service, calls come in that can involve anything from car wrecks and heart attacks to kitchen fires or full warehouse blazes.

Firefighters have to be prepared to handle any type of call, at any time of the day or night. They work odd hours, usually a 24 hour shift, with 48 or 72 hours off between.

Because of the emergencies and traumas these people share, firefighters are very close to their co-workers, who become almost like a close-knit family. Everyone gets a nickname (tag)—some of them are silly or have secret meanings. There's a lot of camaraderie, some good-natured teasing and horseplay, and a lot of concern for one another's welfare, both on and off the job.

Teamwork is the most important aspect of being a firefighter. This is not a job for loners. Lives depend on cooperation and trust. On a team, the nozzle man can't put water on the fire unless the engineer makes it happen, and that doesn't happen unless the mechanic has done his job. Each person has a role to play.

Firefighters live with each other during their shifts. The teamwork has to transfer to the station as well as on calls. If there are social interaction problems—trouble at the dinner table or over what television programs to watch—no matter how good they are in the field, they won't make good team players and they won't last on the job.

Becoming a firefighter

In the past, fire departments would just hire and train you, straight out of high school. The pay was low, it was dangerous work, and not that many people wanted to become firefighters. There is much more competition today, and most fire departments expect you to have undergone training before you even apply for a job. You can take a twelve-week firefighter training program or study in a two-year program for an associate's degree in fire science after graduating from high school. Today, many firefighters also become certified emergency medical technicians through a six-week training course. Once hired, firefighters continue their training, either on their own or through classes.

It is also wise to have good verbal and written skills. Math and chemistry are important, too, and those who want to climb the administrative ladder should take business and management courses.

Firefighters must also have physical and emotional strength. They wear heavy gear and carry heavy equipment and regularly encounter upsetting situations. The ability to cope is a necessity.

It's a good idea to try to get some related experience as early as you can. Volunteer fire departments usually will accept trainees who are still in school. The Boy Scouts of America also has a program to train future firefighters. You can learn more about that at the end of this chapter.

Ranks and divisions

Following is a list of the different divisions you will find in a fire department. Each one is covered in this book.

Operations

Fire and Safety Inspection/Public Education

Fire Investigation

Emergency Medical Services

Training

Administration

No matter what division you work in, you will have a rank. The titles and, sometimes, the specific duties, vary from department to department, but the general responsibilities are the same.

Firefighter: Everyone starts out in this rank. Firefighters do just as their title implies—they fight fires. They might also learn specialties and deal with hazardous materials or medical emergencies.

Engineer: This person is responsible for getting the crew and equipment to the scene. He or she

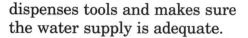

dispenses tools and makes sure the water supply is adequate.

Lieutenant: The lieutenant is responsible for the proper operation of the station during his or her shift, assigning duties, and ensuring the welfare and safety of the crew.

The next three levels, **Battalion Chief/Captain/Division Chief/Commander; Deputy Chief/Assistant Chief;** and **Fire Chief** are covered more fully in the last chapter.

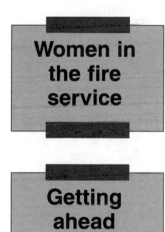

Women in the fire service

Women have played an equal role in the fire service for about the past fifteen years. As firefighters, men and women take the same courses, the same tests, and perform the same duties. Women earn the right to be firefighters just as men do.

Getting ahead

Firefighters can take tests for promotion after about three years. As long as you have the experience and the technical knowledge, you can move up, as long as there's an opening.

The pleasures and pressures of the job

Although the salaries are pretty good these days, most firefighters will tell you that their job is not about money. When you get into the fire service, it's not like a regular job; it's more like answering a calling. Firefighters sacrifice a lot for this calling. They risk their lives and their health.

Let's Meet...

Samantha "Super 12" Kievman

Firefighter

Samantha is a firefighter, an EMT, and a paramedic. She has been with her fire department since 1993. She loves her job and couldn't imagine doing anything else.

What is the firefighter training like?

Training starts first thing in the morning and finishes up at around six in the evening, five days a week for 12 weeks. Every morning you run a mile and a half, do situps, pull ups, and all sorts of other workouts.

You then clean up and go into the classroom. We review something in class; then we go outside and actually do it.

Not everyone makes it through the training program. Sometimes they can't keep up physically or academically. I studied every night. It's exhausting—climbing and lugging heavy dummies and equipment.

What's your job like?

In the fire service, you see it all and you do it all. You meet so many people; you're always surrounded by people. When you pull up on a scene they're really happy to see you.

We go on calls for all sorts of fires—cars, houses, kitchens. We also respond to medical calls—falls or chest pains or car accidents.

You never know what to expect. You have to be on alert for twenty-four hours. No matter what you're doing you have to stop to go on a call. We could have a quiet day, or a day where we're running 24 hours straight.

What do you do at the station when you're not out on a call?

One day a week we clean everything in the kitchen, then another day, we clean out the dorm. On Saturday it's lawn day. If something goes wrong at the station, we fix it. We also have training sessions, and paramedic meetings once a month.

Are there any downsides to your job?

There's a lot of pressure when you pull up on a car accident and you have four victims in bad condition. If someone dies, it's terrible. Although we'd like to, we can't save everybody. If you let it bother you, you can't do your job. You have to have compassion, but you also have to be able to handle the job.

Do you have any advice for someone considering a career as a firefighter?

Go for it! Go to EMT school, paramedic school, fire school, and get as much schooling as you possibly can. The fire service wants people who are willing to give 100 percent. We're dealing with people's lives. Second best is not good enough.

Samantha's First Day on the Job

Samantha's first day on the job was a mixture of excitement and nervousness.

"I remember coming in, not knowing anybody and being so nervous and shy. We go on duty at 7:30 A.M., but I was early. I walked into the bay at 6:55 A.M. I got my gear, went up to a firefighter, and told him I was a new recruit. I asked him where I should go, what I should do.

"I put my gear on the truck and sure enough, right away at 7:35 we got the first call. I remember the tones went off and my heart started jumping. 'Get on the truck,' someone yelled out to me. I hopped on, got all buckled in, and pulled my gloves on. I was so excited, and I was thinking: here I am on a fire truck, I worked so hard to get here and I'm a firefighter now.

"I don't even remember what the call was, only that I asked a lot of questions and stuck close to another firefighter. You're never really alone. But I was so nervous.

"I'm still nervous. You can run the same call over and over, but when the alarms go off your heart rate still increases. No matter how many times you do it, it's always a different situation."

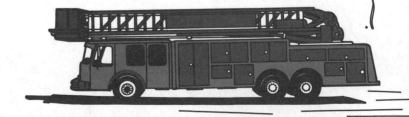

Let's Meet...

Jerry "Psycho" O'Brien
Engineer

Jerry is an engineer and a Haz-Mat (Hazardous Materials) technician. He has been a firefighter since 1982 and has worked for two different fire departments.

How did you get started as a firefighter?

I stumbled upon the fire service by accident. I was managing a retail store when I saw an ad for the fire department. I went through the physical and written testing. I was hired after about a year and a half on the waiting list. Once I got into the fire service, I found out that firefighters study a lot.

How did you move up to engineer?

To become an engineer in most fire departments, you must work at least three years as a firefighter. You study water flow, the equipment, and driving in hazardous conditions.

You take a written test and a practical test. For the practical, you hook up to a hydrant and are given a couple of problems to solve. For example, you're told to stretch an inch-and-three-quarters hose and a two-and-a-half-inch hose

and flow them at the correct water pressures.
You have to be able to go to the pump panel,
make split-second calculations, and operate
the apparatus without overpressuring a line.
The practical portion of the exam is a real
challenge. You need a knowledge of basic
math and algebra and how to use hydraulic
formulas. The flow meters on some of the
newer trucks do a lot of the calculating for
you. Technology has simplified the job.

What are the duties of a driver/engineer?

You have to maintain the apparatus and
equipment, and inspect every piece of equipment every day. All the medical gear and the
tools have to be in a state of readiness; there
must be oil, gas, and water in the truck, and
you have to make sure the hose lines are
correct. You are responsible for transporting
the firefighters, the crew, and all the equipment to whatever assignment is received.

At a fire, you are responsible for supplying
water for the fire suppression—both estab-
lishing enough water coming into the engine
from the hydrant and pumping it out to the
structure. The engineer is also responsible for
dispensing all of the tools on the apparatus;
the axes, pry bars, whatever is needed.

What are the upsides and downsides?

The fun thing about being an engineer is
getting to drive a big truck. I've driven fire
engines in the mountains, on ice, on all kinds
of terrain. And you handle many things at
once. It's a challenge, and at a fire, you get a
good feeling when everything runs smoothly.

Jerry's Most Memorable Fire

The fire Jerry will never forget involved a huge warehouse and an $8 million loss.

"There were approximately 15 fire engines there. I was a driver and the first engine on the scene," Jerry explains. "I arrived to find a literal fire storm. This warehouse was burning intensely. It was picking up pieces of material from the fire and depositing them 4 and 5 miles away. Wherever these pieces landed, they started grass fires all over the city.

"It was the middle of the night, but the entire sky was orange. As we got closer, we saw a thick column of smoke. We were driving through falling fire brands—it was raining fire on us. As we moved closer, I didn't think I was nervous, but I noticed that my foot was bouncing on the accelerator.

"I felt so insignificant seeing how inadequate our big weapons were against this blaze. It was clear that the fire was in control. It took so much water, we drained an entire pond.

"It was an extremely dangerous fire, but there wasn't even one injury. I doubt I'll ever see a fire that big again."

Success Story

In 1945, the U.S. Forest Service launched a campaign to educate Americans about the dangers of forest fires. As part of this effort, Albert Staehle was asked to create a fire prevention symbol. The symbol he created was a forest-dwelling "spokes-mammal," Smokey the Bear.

Five years later, when firefighters walking through the aftermath of a fire in New Mexico's Lincoln National Forest came across a burned and frightened bear cub, it was only natural they named him Smokey.

The cub weighed 4 pounds and was clinging to the smoking remains of a blackened tree. It was a miracle that he survived the fire. The orphaned cub was given a new home at the Smithsonian's National Zoological Park in Washington, D.C., delighting a generation of school-children until his death in 1976.

It is now 50 years since the creation of the legend-ary fire prevention symbol. Old Fur Face (remember, *all* firefighters get nicknames) has shown up on posters, television commercials, billboards, and even a postage stamp. Smokey the Bear is one of the best-loved heroes in our history.

Find Out More

You and firefighting

The Boy Scouts of America has a great program for girls and boys who want to learn about careers in firefighting. Through the Exploring Program, local fire departments work with teens, provide them with uniforms and teach them the basics of firefighting.

Once a week, they meet as a group with professional firefighters who coordinate the program. They get general training in first-aid, fire trucks, and equipment. After they are tested, they are allowed to ride on the trucks as cadets. They are issued fire gear and can go to fires and other emergencies.

Although cadets are not allowed to go into burning buildings, the program is an excellent way to find out what it's really like to be a firefighter.

Cadets can start the program at age 14 and stay in until they are 20 years old. Cadets often are hired as full-time firefighters right out of the program.

Find out more about firefighting

The best way to find out about the Exploring Program in your area is to call your local Boy Scout Council. For general information, write the national office at:

Boy Scouts of America
Exploring Program
P.O. Box 152079
Irving, TX 75015

For information on careers in firefighting contact:

International Association of Fire Fighters
1750 New York Avenue, N.W.
Washington, DC 20006

For an idea about what to expect on firefighting exams, you can take a look at the following book at your library:

Arco Firefighter, by Robert Andriuolo, Deputy Chief, New York City Fire Department, Prentice Hall.

This book will help prepare you for the firefighter exams. It reviews everything you'll need to know, provides sample written and physical fitness tests, and gives tips and strategies for earning high test scores.

FIREFIGHTING

SPECIALISTS

I t would be rare these days to meet a firefighter whose only skill was putting out fires. Personnel must be experts in a variety of techniques. Cross-training helps the fire department get as much of the crew involved in an emergency as needed.

Every emergency requires specific skills. Cross-training is also more cost-effective for the fire department and taxpayers and is more interesting for all firefighters.

15

The paths you can take

Once on the force, you have a number of options open to you, and you don't have to be promoted to driver/engineer or lieutenant to take advantage of them. To be on a specialist team, you first must exhibit a desire to do the work. Then, an opening must exist on a particular team. Even more important, the team has to feel you would be a good addition.

Each team requires certain training or skills. Here is a list of the different specialty teams you could train for:

Extrication Specialist: These specialists learn to operate the Jaws of Life, a valuable tool for rescuing victims trapped in car wrecks.

High-Angle Rescue: These rescuers use ropes and ladders and work at heights above two stories. They can rappel off tall buildings where ladders won't reach, climb up on water tanks, or down dangerous cliffsides.

Hazardous Materials Technician: This specialty is commonly known as Haz-Mat. Haz-Mat technicians are familiar with all types of chemicals and their containers.

Technical Rescue: This includes underground rescue in confined spaces. Urban search and rescue specialists find people in the aftermath of hurricanes or earthquakes. Technical rescuers also know how to pull out a dog or other animal trapped in a well or drainpipe.

Underwater Rescue: Underwater rescue teams are trained to dive in the ocean, in lakes, and into dark canals. They know how to operate with zero visibility, feeling their way along the bottom with their hands, searching for a submerged car or body.

Emergency Medical Services: Emergency medical technicians and paramedics help in all sorts of medical emergencies.

What it's like being a specialist firefighter

Specialist firefighters are a part of the regular combat firefighting team. They are prepared, just as every firefighter is, to answer whatever calls come into the station. Not surprisingly, many firefighters are expert in more than one specialty area.

The training for firefighting specialists

The amount and type of training for each specialty varies. Let's look at each area again and see what's involved:

Extrication Specialist: Those interested in this specialty take courses and seminars offered by rescue equipment manufacturers, learn on-the-job, or practice on junk cars on their own time. They must be familiar with levers and hydraulics and understand automobile construction, knowing where both the weak and strong points are.

High-Angle Rescue: The specialized skills used in high-angle rescues are learned through local fire academies or community colleges and through on-the-job training.

Hazardous Materials Technician: Haz-Mat trainees study the behavior of chemicals that are spilled or involved in a fire. They learn to use heat detectors and monitors. They also use computers to help research and identify different chemicals. Programs are offered through fire academies, community colleges, and through continuing education courses given at individual fire departments.

Technical Rescue: Techniques for technical rescues are taught in fire academies, community college fire science programs, and during in-house continuing education training.

Underwater Rescue: These experts are all trained as certified divers. They have to be expert swimmers first, with strength and endurance. In addition to the skills every scuba diver learns, underwater rescue divers must know how to work in pitch black conditions, freezing water, or in dangerous rapids or heavy surf conditions.

Emergency Medical Services: EMTs can learn their skills in a six-week course. Paramedics can spend up to two years in training before becoming certified. Programs are usually offered through community colleges. To keep their certification current, emergency medical service workers must participate in continuing education classes.

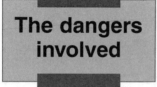

The dangers involved

Each specialty has its own risks, on top of those shared by all firefighters. Haz-Mat specialists have the added risk of exposure to dangerous chemicals and vapors. EMTs and paramedics can come into contact with contagious diseases. Underwater divers risk exposure to the cold and drowning. High-angle rescuers can fall, and technical rescuers can become trapped under collapsing walls and roofs.

The danger is there and it's very real, but instead of scaring off the men and women mentioned here, it seems to be the very thing that attracts them to the job.

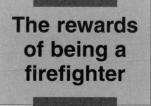

The rewards of being a firefighter

As you will see mentioned throughout this book, the main reward of firefighting is the challenge and the excitement. Firefighters do not like sitting behind desks. They want to be on the cutting edge, totally involved in life-threatening situations. But the greatest reward is having helped someone.

Let's Meet...

Paul "Cid" Ceresa
Hazardous Materials Specialist

Paul has been a firefighter for almost 20 years. He is an EMT, a trainer, and a Haz-Mat specialist, but what he loves most of all is being a nozzle man and fighting fires.

How did you get started with the fire department?

I started as a volunteer when I was 14 years old, and fell in love with it. My grandfather had been a fire chief. It's not unusual to see the children and grandchildren of firefighters go on to become firefighters, too.

Tell us about the Haz-Mat field.

Hazardous materials is part of firefighting, too. Because our society is involved with so many chemicals, materials exist that are extremely flammable, poisonous, or radioactive.

We started learning to deal with these chemicals about 15 years ago. A new discipline, Haz-Mat, was created.

How do you deal with a dangerous chemical accident?

We have to know all about chemistry. We also have to study the containers that different materials are kept in. We have a lot of technology that goes into this—heat detectors and all sorts of monitors.

First we have to identify the product. This can be difficult. Once you've identified what you're dealing with, if it's a gas, you assess wind direction and speed. You factor in other environmental conditions, such as humidity. If the chemical is flammable, you eliminate possible sources of ignition so an explosion will not occur.

If we have to go in, we dress our team in the proper gear to give us chemical and thermal protection. We use hose streams to help control a leak or build dams.

Luckily, these accidents don't happen all the time. In our fire department, we respond about 450 times a year. Sometimes it's just 10 gallons of gasoline spilled in someone's garage. I'm not saying that it's not dangerous; it's just more routine. Last week we were called in for 3,700 gallons of a strong acid that leaked from a wastewater treatment plant.

What do you need to know to work with hazardous materials?

There are five levels of Haz-Mat training. First is the awareness level; learning how to identify the product. Next is the operational level, which teaches you how to deal defensively with hazardous materials. For example, we might make a dam to contain the spill, never touching the product.

The third level is for the technician who has had about 140 to 200 hours of training. At this level, you learn how to enter the accident area safely. The Haz-Mat specialist is the next level. He or she has a lot more training and learns about the field in much more detail. Then there are Haz-Mat incident commanders who have additional training and supervise an operation.

A Trust Rebuilt

One of the rules of firefighting is that you never abandon your partner. But one day Paul was left in a fire by himself. His partner ran out of air and took off, leaving Paul.

"I wouldn't have left without him," Paul explains. "I was angry with him for years and wouldn't hook up with him on a hose line again.

"Years later, we were fighting a huge fire in an apartment building. He was on one hose line, and I was on another. We were working our way down the hallway. One crew stayed in the hallway, holding the fire back, and the other crew did forceful entry into each room.

"Suddenly the fire came right at us. A lot of the crew got burned and ran out. When everything cleared, we were the only two left.

"He got pretty burned, but he stayed. After that I was able to trust him again. And I realized I had been wrong for judging him on one mistake. All of us make mistakes.

"Now, I'd fight a fire with that guy any day."

Let's Meet...

Rob "Bubba" Brantley

Extrication Specialist

Rob had always wanted to be a firefighter; in fact, no other job possibility had ever crossed his mind. He is also an EMT and is part of several other specialty teams.

What kind of calls do you go out on?

I go out on fires—houses or cars or boats. You can't imagine the different things that can catch on fire. Warehouses are the most dangerous because you don't know what's inside. It could be gunpowder or chemicals.

I also go out on any kind of auto accident. We go there to stabilize the situation and remove any danger to life or property. For example, if a car crashes into a house and the car is burning, we try to get the car out of the way so the house doesn't catch on fire, too.

We also do medical and other types of rescues. But we don't often rescue cats from trees. If you think about it, you don't often see cat skeletons in trees. They always manage to get down by themselves.

We've rescued quite a few pelicans out of trees, though. They get caught in fishing lines, then fly up into the trees, and the line gets caught.

Tell us about your specialty.

Working the Jaws of Life is my favorite
thing to do. If someone is in trouble at a
wreck, I like to feel I can get them out faster
than anyone. I've spent a lot of time practic-
ing taking cars apart.

To be an extrication specialist, you need
common sense and you need to know about
leverage and about how different parts of cars
react to pressure. There are parts of a car that
are weaker than others. You have to know
where and how to cut. You have to know how
to take windshields out without getting glass
all over everybody. Safety is the key. You don't
want to hurt the person in the car anymore
than he or she has already been hurt.

Also, there's a time factor. They call it the
Golden Hour. Basically you have one hour to
get someone out of a wreck and to a trauma
center to increase the chances of survival.
We have to know how to act fast.

**How does someone learn to become an
extrication specialist?**

First, the crew has to have confidence in
you. The work is dangerous, so you don't
want someone with you who's going to panic.
If that happens you'll have one more person
to rescue.

You can go out of your way to practice.
You can tell your supervisor you'd like to go
to the junkyard and practice taking cars
apart. I went to some seminars, but most of
my training is from general knowledge. I
worked with hydraulics before I got on the
fire department. If you want training, most
departments will train you.

A Dream Come True

Rob Brantley was like many other kids; he was fascinated by old fire trucks and all their fancy accessories. He used to see an old truck sitting abandoned in a field and he dreamed of one day owning it. The truck had been the city's very first fire truck, a 1926 American LaFrance.

"As I grew up I forgot about it," Rob explains. "The city had sold it and it was no longer around. Then I started working as a firefighter for the city. A group of us—firefighters and interested citizens—formed a restoration society. We located the truck and bought it with the understanding that no single person would ever own the truck. We wanted to restore it and preserve it as a museum piece.

"We took it all apart, sandblasted it and completely restored everything. I'm still working on it.

"It's been great. It's been a way to own that truck I admired as a kid. I take it on parades, ride in it as Santa Claus or go to functions for disabled kids and brighten their day a little bit. It's a real dream come true."

Success Story

Fire Equipment: Past and Present

Firefighting has come a long way over the centuries. It is now a high-tech field utilizing state-of-the-art fire and rescue equipment. But it wasn't always that way. Later in this book you will read about one method of fighting fires, passing along leather buckets filled with water. Water supplies came from tanks of stored rainwater and later from draining reservoirs or ponds. Rival volunteer fire companies used to fight over the water supply, so fire companies started hiring prizefighters to guard the water.

Fire hydrants connected to city water supplies weren't invented until 1801. Early fire hoses were made of stitched-together leather, but they leaked and could not withstand much pressure. Rubber hoses were first used in 1871, in Cincinnati. Ladders were used as early as 1200 A.D. by the cliff dwellers of New Mexico. During Colonial times, ladders were often mounted on the outside of people's homes, near their leather buckets. Today, most departments use a variety of ladders, including aerial ladders, operated hydraulically.

As society becomes more complex, so does the need for more complex equipment. The Jaws of Life was first developed to free men trapped in race cars. It was quickly adapted for use with fire/rescue companies. It's a hydraulic tool that can spread the frame of a car apart. Some are portable; others are permanent fixtures on squad trucks, powered by the engine's motor.

Find Out More

You and firefighting

Firefighters are take-charge people. They act and react quickly. What kind of person are you?

Here's a little quiz to help you evaluate yourself.

It's early Sunday morning and you are driving down the highway. There are very few cars on the road at this hour so you are surprised to come across a three-car pileup on the other side of the road. It must have just happened because no one else has stopped yet. It looks pretty bad; there's broken glass everywhere and what appears to be blood.

What would you do?

1. You say to yourself as you drive past, "Oh, isn't that terrible. I hope no one was hurt too badly."

2. You pull over and jump out of your car and start trying to wave down passing vehicles. You feel your throat go raw from screaming for someone to help.

3. You cross the road and make
    your way to the first car, then
    check the other two vehicles.
    You figure that someone will
    pass with a car phone and call
    911. Meanwhile, you have
    three injured people to calm
    down and help.

Did you choose #3? If so, it
looks as if you're investigating the
right career.

EMERGENCY MEDICAL SERVICES

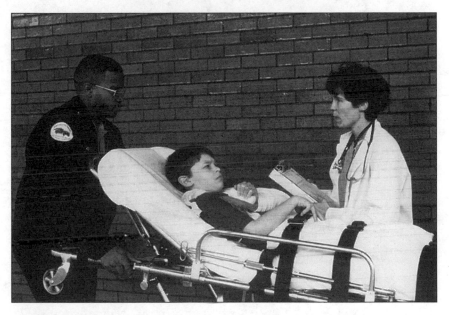

These days more and more fire departments across the country have combined firefighting with rescue services. As a result, each fire department has to make sure a large number, if not all, of its firefighters are also trained emergency medical technicians and paramedics.

If you want to help people and you have a strong interest in the medical field, a career as a firefighting EMT or paramedic could be right for you.

Emergency medical technicians and paramedics

Emergency medical technicians, or EMTs, know the basics of first aid and life-saving. They learn CPR, patient handling, extrication, and the basics of medical illnesses and medical injuries.

EMTs provide basic life-support. They are expected to arrive on the scene and take care of a patient until the paramedics arrive. If the EMTs and paramedics arrive together, the EMT assists the paramedic. An EMT might also be responsible for driving the ambulance.

A paramedic has to be an EMT first. Paramedics are trained in very sophisticated, advanced levels of life-support. Their goal is to keep a patient alive, and they function in the field as an extension to a physician. They are the pre-hospital hands, eyes, and ears of the doctor and have to be able to assess a situation and react the way a doctor would. Paramedics have a strong relationship with physicians, who have learned over time to trust the paramedics' training and expertise.

The duties and the limitations of an EMT

Although EMTs perform very valuable services to patients in the field, statistics have shown that the more advanced the forms of treatment, the better are the patient's chances of survival. This is why paramedical training beyond the EMT level was begun.

For example, if someone has a cardiac arrest at home, the EMT can go to the house, start CPR, put the patient on a stretcher, give oxygen and hope the patient pulls through. With only a four to six minute grace period before the brain becomes permanently damaged from lack of oxygen, the actions of the EMT help, but in many cases, are not enough.

The paramedic can function in the field the way the doctor would in the emergency room. Paramedics can defibrillate, oxygenate, and administer some drugs right on the spot. The less time the patient spends not breathing, the higher are the chances of recovery. Paramedics strive to deliver fast and effective intervention.

What's it really like?—The excitement and the stress

As an EMT or paramedic in a fire department you work shifts just as the firefighters do. The most common is 24 hours on with 48 hours off.

When you're not out on a call, you spend your time at the fire station with your co-workers. But you can never really relax. You'll always be waiting for the alarms to go off.

When you hear the tones, you run for the truck and get in as quickly as possible. If you're driving, you have to know where you're going, and if you don't know the area well, you must be able to read maps. There's a lot of pressure to get to the scene fast. If you waste time, you can lose lives.

When you get to the scene, you'll see people waving; you'll see police and crowds. One of the stresses is realizing they're all waiting for you. When you get out of the truck, all eyes are on you. You can't afford to look frightened or uncertain. You're expected to have a good idea of what's wrong and to do the right thing.

You work hard and quickly to stabilize the victims and having done that, you get them to the hospital. On the way you call ahead so the hospital expects you.

You never know who the patient will be. You might have to deal with drunk or hostile people or situations that are potentially violent. Sometimes you think you're going on a call for someone who is sick, but when you get there it turns out to be something else—maybe someone who is acting crazy, waving a gun around. Sometimes police are there to help you; sometimes they're busy and can't help you. Sometimes an EMT or paramedic is killed in the line of duty.

The rewards come from helping people and saving lives. But it's not just the major incidents that are satisfying. Sometimes it's the small things. Sometimes people are scared, and making them feel better makes you feel better.

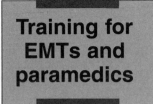

Training for EMTs and paramedics

EMTs can generally be trained in six to twelve weeks, through a community college. During the course of their program, they spend time observing in hospitals and gain practical experience riding in an ambulance. To become certified, EMTs are given a practical exam through the school and a written exam through the state.

Once you have become a certified EMT, you can go on to paramedic school. Most programs are offered through community colleges. The training for a paramedic could take anywhere from one to two years.

Paramedic trainees also spend a lot of time in hospitals learning advanced techniques. They spend time in operating rooms and on hospital critical care floors, learning how to take care of patients.

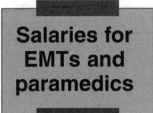

Salaries for EMTs and paramedics

EMTs working for a private ambulance company in a small town make as little as $5 to $10 an hour. But, as a firefighter *and* EMT, the salary ranges from $25,000 to $38,000 a year, depending upon the area of the country. As experience increases, those figures can rise.

Paramedics working outside a fire department could make anywhere from $12,000 to $20,000 a year. Combined paramedic/firefighters generally start in the mid to high 20s, and can go as high as $50,000 or more per year.

Let's Meet...

Tania Maxwell
Emergency Medical Technician

Becoming a firefighter had been Tania's childhood dream. She has been an EMT since 1989 and plans to study to become a paramedic. She loves being able to help other people.

What drew you to the profession?

My neighbor was the chief of my hometown fire department. As a kid I used to see his truck in the neighborhood, in front of his house, and it fascinated me. He talked to me about the profession, and inspired and encouraged me.

Tell us about being an EMT. What's it like?

EMTs help the paramedics, making their job easier. We do basic life-saving, CPR when necessary, apply bandages, get the medications for the paramedics to administer—all the basics. We're involved in everything related to saving lives.

What's it like being a woman in the fire department? Do the men give you a hard time?

I think that after doing this job for more than seven years, I've proven myself. I am able to do my job and do it effectively; but at the beginning, I felt I had to work harder. The guys didn't make me feel that way, it was all me. They're like my big brothers. They look out for me and make sure nothing happens to me. Everything operates on the buddy system. You know that your big brother is right there with you.

What do you like most about your work?

What I enjoy most is being around the people. After the paramedics have done their work and taken the patient to the hospital, as an EMT I get to stay around and talk to the family, explain what we're doing and reassure them that we have some of the best paramedics in the state and in the nation.

Are there any downsides?

Yes, when there's nothing you can do. Where I live we have a lot of swimming pools and drownings. The worst part is being called to rescue a child who was left unattended and has fallen into the pool. You do everything you possibly can, but sometimes it's still not enough.

But I try to think about the flip side; that it's always joyful to bring a life into this world when we deliver a new baby. We save a lot more lives than we lose.

Any advice for a young person considering a career as an EMT?

Be the very best at whatever you choose to do, whether it's firefighter, EMT, or paramedic, and remember that hard work and perseverance make everything go well. If the mind can perceive it, you can achieve it. If you think big enough, you can do anything.

A Life Saved, A Friend Made

Tania was called to a home where a woman was very depressed. She was contemplating suicide.

"She was an older woman and personal problems had really taken their toll on her," Tania remembers. "She had gotten a divorce and had lost a lot of things in the divorce. Along with the material things, she had lost her self-esteem.

"I sat and talked with her for over an hour and a half, trying to let her know that everything was going to be okay.

"Afterwards, we got her counseling, then later she called and I got a letter from her. She thanked me for letting her know that every cloud has a silver lining. Every day she finds something new to live for. She calls me her little guardian angel.

"She still sends me letters. I write her back and if it gets tough, she calls me. Whenever I look back on this incident, I see a reason to do what I do. To me it didn't seem like a whole lot, but to her, it was her life."

Let's Meet...

Lieutenant Woodrow "Woody" Poitier
Paramedic

Woody Poitier became a paramedic before becoming a firefighter. He was in the first group of paramedics his city hired when the program was started.

What are your duties as a paramedic?

My main duty is to preserve life. Whenever we're called for an emergency, we try to take care of the problem. Every call is different.

I also function as a paramedic supervisor. The paramedic supervisor only goes on certain calls; normally those that involve trauma or calls involving children. My job is to make sure the call is handled properly.

In addition to emergency calls, there are reports that have to be written. We also have to stock the truck and make sure the equipment is always ready to go. There's an assignment to take care of every day.

What's it like being a paramedic?

I've delivered about 14 babies, most of them in the back of ambulances on the interstate. One lady named her child after me. I've also worked shootings, stabbings, cuttings, drownings, and more.

I've seen calls where everything has gone right—we have dynamite paramedics on the scene—yet the victim can't be saved. Other times, everything seems to go wrong; you can't get an IV started, nothing seems to be working, and yet the patient lives.

There's no rhyme or reason. I do know that paramedics do a good job. Even if you can help only one person in a 24 hour period, it is worth it.

What do you like most and what do you like least about your job?

It's satisfying work. I like being able to help people. Every emergency is different. When you come into people's homes and their lives, the positive energy you put in always seems to have a positive result. That's really, really rewarding.

We go out on a lot of calls. Most of them are legitimate, but a lot of them are not. These are calls we don't deem as emergency calls; the guy who's had a toothache for three days and decides to call you at three o'clock in the morning because he can't fall asleep, and he wants you to do something— or the guy who stubbed his toe. Some people feel that if they call us and go to the hospital on a stretcher, they'll be treated more quickly in the emergency room.

Do you have any advice for future paramedics?

If you want a rewarding job and one that actually helps people, this is the job to go into. But you have to stay in school.

Some Kind of Miracle

The call came in about 6:30 in the evening. Two little boys, about eight or nine years old, were playing near a substation belonging to the power company. They climbed a fence and one of them, not realizing the danger, grabbed onto a transformer. He immediately took 7,900 volts and suffered third degree burns all over his entire body.

The call to 911 was made. Woody explains what happened next: "When we got there we pulled up to the fence, and we could see the kid lying on the ground. He appeared to be dead.

"We climbed the fence and saw that he was breathing, but his heart was beating very erratically. We put a heart monitor on him, gave him oxygen, started IV lines, treated some of his burns, and rushed him to the hospital where they were able to stabilize him.

"The electricity had gone in through his hands and had come out through his feet. No one should have been able to survive that, but he did. I've seen a lot less voltage kill someone. It was a miracle."

Success Story

Whenever there's a natural disaster—earthquakes, floods, hurricanes, etc.—at home, or in some far-away country, the Red Cross always seems to be the first relief organization on the scene. And in countries torn by war, the Red Cross is always there to help the victims.

The men and women who work for the Red Cross are brave and dedicated health professionals. By maintaining a political neutrality, they are able to enter countries in conflict. But even though the red cross painted on rooftops and flown on flags is supposed to warn away any hostile armies, they are still targets.

Jean Henri Dunant, from Switzerland, founded the International Red Cross in 1863. Clara Barton founded the American Red Cross in 1881.

In addition to natural disasters and war relief, the Red Cross teaches courses in first aid and water safety, helps refugees, and maintains blood banks.

Find Out More

You and emergency medical services

In high school, you will find that your school probably offers a health occupations program that will allow you to get a taste of all the different medical paths you could follow.

Students in this program take medical skills classes in the tenth grade. In the eleventh grade (or the twelfth—it's up to you when you take the program), students spend 36 weeks studying medical courses, going on field trips to hospitals and community centers, and riding with ambulances or fire/rescue trucks. By the time you finish, you will know if being a paramedic, a doctor, or an emergency room nurse would be the career you'd prefer.

This program is open to all students dedicated to pursuing a career in health occupations. Students in this program must also be members of Health Occupations Students of America (HOSA).

For more information, contact your high school's guidance counselor or health occupations teacher, or write to:

HOSA
6309 N. O'Connor Rd., Suite 215
    LB117
Irving, TX 75039-3510

Find out more about emergency medical services

General information about EMTs and paramedics is available from:

National Association of
    Emergency Medical
    Technicians
9140 Ward Parkway
Kansas City, MO 64114

Information concerning training courses, registration, and job opportunities can be obtained by writing to the State Emergency Medical Service Director, listed in your phone book.

The Red Cross offers courses in basic first aid and CPR. You can find an office near you by looking in your phone book. The address for their national headquarters is:

American Red Cross
National Headquarters
17th & D Streets, N.W.
Washington, DC 20006

FIRE
INVESTIGATION
AND PREVENTION

Fire investigators arrive at the scene of a fire and try to determine how it started. Fire inspectors make sure that all buildings are constructed with an eye on fire safety. Public safety educators talk to children and adults about how to prevent future fires.

If you have an inquiring nature or would love to share your knowledge with the public, a career as a fire investigator, fire inspector, or public safety educator might be the right path for you.

What fire investigation is all about

Although there are many types of fires, they all fall into just two categories: accidental or criminal.

An accident happens when someone falls asleep smoking a cigarette, or oily rags left in a corner suddenly ignite. Criminal fires are fires that were set on purpose. This is called arson and is punishable by law. Fires caused by bombs also fall under the category of criminal fires.

Fire investigators check into both accidental and criminal fires. The engine company first goes out and does the firefighting. Once the fire has been put out, the lieutenant on the scene will take a look at it to see if he understands why the fire started. He will include this information in his written report. If the loss is above $5,000, or there is a suspicion that the fire wasn't accidental, the fire investigator comes in to do a more in-depth check.

How the fire investigator gets the job done

Fire investigators look at fires as big puzzles with lots of little pieces that have to be put together in order to make sense.

The fire investigator likes to be at the scene when the fire is still burning. A fire in progress can give a lot of information. Sometimes he or she can tell from the color of the flame or the smoke what caused the fire.

Watching how the fire reacts to water also gives some clues. If the fire doesn't go right out when soaked with water, if it keeps coming back, there's a good chance fuel was used.

After the fire is out, everything looks black, but the debris still reveals clues. Investigators can shovel through the mess and look for burn patterns. They can see which side of a piece of wood or what part of the carpeting is more deeply burned.

They look at wiring, fuse boxes, and circuit-breaker boxes. They also talk to the firefighters and ask what they saw. Were the doors unlocked? Was anyone running away? Was there broken glass lying inside or was it blown outside by the fire?

The dangers Involved

These days many materials in our homes are made from plastic, and plastic is made with chemicals. After a fire, when the temperature cools down, the fumes start escaping. Because of this, fire investigators must wear masks with filters to protect their lungs.

Shoveling through the debris in a burned-out building is also dangerous. A fire weakens all the structure's supports and roofs can collapse, walls can cave in, and floors can give way.

The pleasures and the pressures of the job

Fire inspectors get their satisfaction from figuring out how fires started. They like to be able to look back and say that they know now that the toaster oven went bad or someone broke into the house and poured gasoline on the carpet.

But the frustration comes from not being able to prove who did it and to see the arsonist caught. Critical evidence often gets destroyed in the fire.

Fire safety, prevention, and public education

Some firefighters work with builders and contractors, helping them to make sure their construction complies with safety standards. For new construction, they go over the blueprints with the builder. For existing property, they make periodic visits to conduct their inspections. Some of the things they look for are faulty wiring, poor ventilation, not enough exits, or the overuse of extension cords.

All firefighters would like the public to know how to prevent needless fires from happening. Some firefighters choose to work as public safety educators. They start with young children and teach them important, lifesaving tips.

Working with the law

Fire investigators and fire inspectors sometimes have to work with the police or testify in court. Fire investigators give evidence in court to try to prove when a fire was started for criminal reasons.

They also go to court when a builder refuses to comply with proper safety codes.

Both of these professions require knowledge of the law and court procedure, as well as good writing skills, because their reports might be read in court.

Training for fire investigators and inspectors

Fire investigators must first go through regular firefighter training and put in their time as firefighters. Once you become an investigator, the training is an ongoing process. You'll study fire behavior, chemistry, court procedures, and how to handle evidence. You'll also attend special classes at colleges and fire academies, and train with seasoned investigators.

Not all fire investigators work for fire departments, though. Some, with the appropriate training and experience, find work with insurance companies or private investigation firms.

Fire inspectors must be familiar with building codes and permit laws. While working as a firefighter, they can take additional classes at a community college or fire academy. A fire inspection course of study runs about five weeks.

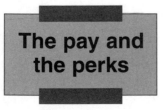

The pay and the perks

The salaries for these different specialties vary. In some departments, inspectors and investigators who carry a firefighter rank earn the same pay and benefits as a firefighter.

Let's Meet...

Robert "Bob" Lemons
Fire Investigator and
Holly
Accelerant Detection Canine

Holly's vocabulary covers only woof, arf, and sometimes snuffle-snuffle, so we talked with her handler, fire investigator Bob Lemons. Holly lives with Bob and his family.

How did you get started in fire investigation?

Once I was on the fire department, I got a broader view of what goes on. I watched the investigators come in at a fire, and I was interested in their work, so I asked a lot of questions.

How did Holly get started?

I saw a magazine article about accelerate detection canines. These dogs have only been around since 1988. I spoke to the chief and said I wanted to attend the Maine State Police Canine Academy, for five weeks, with a dog, to learn how to investigate fires.

He thought that was the funniest thing he'd ever heard. But I showed him the article, did some more research, found out the success rate, and then went back to my chief. He realized a dog like Holly would be a good tool.

What makes Holly a good accelerant detection canine?

I looked at several dogs before I found Holly. You want a dog who is very social, who likes to be around people. She has to be curious and have a good nose. She can't be afraid of loud noises, new environments, or places where the footing isn't always sturdy.

What are Holly's duties?

Holly is trained to go in after a fire and search for residue of a flammable or combustible liquid such as gasoline or lighter fluid. When she finds something, she sits and signals us. We collect the samples from where she's indicated and send them to the lab. Her success rate is very good. Even if the equipment can't pick it up, Holly can.

How does Holly know what to do?

Holly has been trained on a food reward system. The only time she eats is when she finds something. Now that doesn't mean she goes without her regular meals if there are no fires to investigate. On her days off I take a little dropper of flammable liquid the chemist has prepared and put a few drops down, in the driveway, or in my house. Then I have her search for the scent. When she finds it, she gets to eat.

There's a good reason why we use a food reward. A lot of dogs are rewarded with play time. But in a fire setting, all that playing would disturb the evidence. We need a dog that will alert us by sitting very still.

The 5 Steps to Holly's Training

Bob explains how he and Holly went through the training together.

1. First, through repetition, we imprint-ed Holly with the odor. Just as you teach a dog to sit, Holly was taught that when she smells this odor she'll get fed. We start with an odor con-tained in a can; but so she doesn't sit down every time she sees a can, we also put out empty cans.

2. Then we put in a two-step passive alert—the 'sit' and 'show me.' Holly learns to find the odor, then sit. She comes in, sniffs around the can, sits down, and then I say 'show me.' Holly will put her nose exactly where she smells the odor.

3. Now, instead of containing the odor in cans, we put it on the can lids, which we spread out on the ground, so she learns to check on the floor.

4. Next we take her to both "hot" fire scenes, where we know she will find something, and "cold" fire scenes, where we know she won't. We want to make sure she understands she won't always find something every time she comes to a fire scene.

5. Finally, Holly has to pass a test to make sure she really is finding the odor. All her training paid off—Holly passed her test, and has been a member of the investigation team ever since.

Let's Meet...

Lieutenant Roseann Strippoli
Fire Prevention Officer

Roseann works in the fire prevention division of her fire department and is a state certified fire inspector. She learned all the basics of firefighting, but she started right away in fire prevention.

What are your duties?

My job has two major parts to it. As a fire inspector, I have to make sure that people who apply for building permits meet all the safety codes. I inspect the buildings during and after construction, and check out their fire alarms and sprinkler systems.

I'm also involved with safety education. With young children, I cover the basics. What do you do if your clothes should ever catch on fire? The "Stop, Drop, and Roll" drill. I teach them to get down on the floor and crawl if there's a lot of smoke.

We also talk about having fire drills at home, making sure their smoke detectors are working, and not playing with fire, of course.

What's your job like?

It's well suited to me. It's always different. It doesn't get boring like a desk job. I'm either dealing with contractors or going out to schools.

I don't know what my day is going to be like until I get my

assignments. I work 8 to 5, which is good for me as a single mom. I've been with the department for more than 13 years, and during that time, I've only spent the night at the station twice, just to see what it was like.

I also ride on the engine once a month to maintain my skill level. It's good to go on calls. It helps you bond with and trust the people you're working with. I feel like part of a family.

Are there any downsides to your job?

Sometimes the people you deal with in the public are difficult. When I give builders the fire safety requirements or have to tell them something negative, they take it personally.

They don't understand; they don't see what I see. To them it's an inconvenience or it will cost them thousands of dollars to meet the codes. I'm looking out for their own safety, but they don't see that.

What do you like most about your job?

I like working with the kids. The exciting part is when I see the kids get excited. They love it when they're taught something they didn't know. Even if they already do know, they put their hands up and can't wait to tell me about it.

What I like most is that at the end of the day, even if I'm really tired and have had a bad day, I know what I've done is worthwhile. No matter how small the accomplishment was or how much a contractor or builder might have yelled at me or not liked me that day, I still may have made a difference.

What Would You Do If...?

Here are some "What would you do if?" questions Roseann asks the older students she visits.

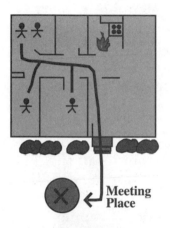

Meeting Place

Q. What would happen if you were sleeping, the smoke detector went off, everyone got out, but went to a different place? What would your parents do if they couldn't find you?

A. They might be scared and may try to go back in. To avoid this, plan a meeting place ahead of time.

Q. What if you were trapped in a room on the second or third floor?

A. It's a good idea to buy a folding ladder that you can store under your bed. If you should need it, the ladder will hook to your window and you can climb down. If you don't have a ladder, first put a sheet or blanket or towel under the door to help stop the smoke from coming in. Then, if there's a phone in the room, call 911.

After that, quickly go to the window, open it and breathe fresh air. Let a sheet hang out the window so the fire rescuers can see where you are.

Success Story

Accelerant Detection Canines are not the only dogs important to the fire service. Dalmatians once played a very important role. In the days of horse-drawn fire engines, dalmatians would trot alongside the vehicle, prompting the horses, and keeping other dogs away.

Dalmatians are short-haired, white dogs with distinctive black or dark brown spots. It is believed that the breed originally came from Dalmatia, in the Balkans, where it was used mainly as a hunting dog. In the mid-1800s, the breed was brought to England and became known there as a carriage dog, keeping pace with horse and buggies or riding on the seat next to the driver.

Dalmatians in the United States, often nicknamed "Sparky," became a long-time symbol of the fire department, long after their working role was over. It's not unusual to find dalmatians kept as pets and mascots in various fire stations around the country.

Find Out More

You and fire investigation

Here are some interesting facts about arson:

Only about four percent of arsonists ever get caught and convicted.

Often, an arsonist will stay near the fire to watch the firefighters at work.

There are several different motives for arson: spite, revenge, anger, and fraud.

The most common kind of arson fraud is when someone's business is going bad and they decide to "sell it back to the insurance company." They hire someone to burn it or burn it themselves, and then try to collect on their insurance.

Another Way To Catch an Arsonist

You just learned about all the things Holly was trained to do. Here's another valuable skill she has.

Bob can take Holly on a leash and walk her through the crowd watching the fire. If the arsonist is hanging around, Holly will be able to find him because he will still have the smell of gasoline on his hands and clothes.

Bob will take her through quickly and when he sees that she's getting ready to alert, he'll pull her away so they don't tip off the arsonist. Bob will then signal the police who will be watching from nearby. They've been able to make quite a few arrests this way. All the arsonist knows is that a dog walked by and a few seconds later the police are on him.

Find out more about fire investigation

For information about professional qualifications and a list of two- and four-year degree programs in fire science or fire prevention contact:

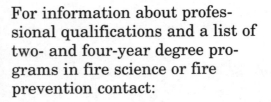

National Fire Protection
    Association
Batterymarch Park
Quincy, MA 02269

TRAINERS

There are many opportunities for firefighters who also love to teach. In addition to programs offered in community colleges and at local and regional fire academies, most fire departments have their own in-house training division.

If you should discover after becoming a firefighter that sharing information and techniques comes naturally to you, you should consider a career as a firefighter trainer.

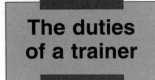

The duties of a trainer

Trainers work with firefighters during various stages of the firefighters' careers. Once someone has decided to become a firefighter, a trainer is almost always the first person he or she encounters. Trainers work with recruits who have no knowledge or experience of the profession, providing them all of the basics.

Trainers teaching the basics of firefighting do not always work inside traditional classrooms. They could take their students into a smoke-filled room to simulate actual fire conditions, or pack them onto a variety of squad trucks and let them get a feel for what actual calls are like.

Trainers also work with seasoned firefighters, helping them keep their skills current or teaching them about new equipment or techniques as they are developed. Trainers are also needed for all those different specialties that firefighters pursue—Haz-Mat and emergency medical services, for example.

There are even trainers who work with animals as well as people. Right now there are only three canine academies—in Maine, Connecticut, and New Jersey—that train accelerant detection dogs like Holly, the fire investigating dog we met previously, but jobs in this specialized area do occasionally open up.

The skills a trainer provides

Here is a list of some of the basics that firefighter trainers must teach:

Building construction: How a building is constructed and how it will react in a fire.

Safety equipment: The bunker gear, the self-contained breathing apparatus—how they work and what their limitations are.

Chemistry: How different materials will react in a fire or if allowed to escape their containers. Firefighters also need to learn how dangerous chemicals can absorb through the skin.

Search patterns: How to search a building for victims in both clear and under zero-visibility conditions.

Rescue techniques: How to use ropes and other equipment and techniques to rescue victims.

Ladders: How to properly place a ladder; how to fight fires from a ladder; how to rescue from a ladder.

Water application: How to lay hose, how to use hose streams to put out a fire, how to pump the water, how to best apply the water, and what will happen after you apply the water.

Teamwork: How to work with and fit into a team.

Most trainers will tell you the hardest part is training people to work as a team. Being part of a team means you are responsible for all the other team members as well as for yourself.

How to become a trainer

Once you are a firefighter, the basic requirement for becoming a trainer is to pass just one training course in classroom methodology. But to take that course, you will need approximately 5 years on the job and a strong background or expertise in your subject area, whether it's hazardous materials, emergency medical services or some other firefighting specialty.

Most trainers take more than one course, however. They can spend many hours studying their specialty.

Here are some of the courses trainers take:

Methods of classroom teaching

Methods of classroom preparation

The use of videos in the classroom

How to use training materials

How to prepare a training outline and training objectives

Evaluation and testing

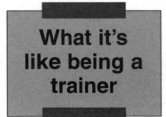

What it's like being a trainer

Some trainers, those who work at fire academies, for example, work full-time and stay with their students for eight to ten hours a day, five days a week. Others work on a part-time basis as a side duty to their regular role as a firefighter.

You might move between different departments, without having a permanent office or classroom. Some trainers even travel to different fire departments around the country.

The time trainers spend in the classroom is only part of their job. Preparing for each class could double the amount of time spent as a trainer.

The rewards, the pay, and the perks

Salaries are determined by the institution that employs you and the number of hours you work. Part-time instructors could earn a minimum hourly wage of $20. Full-time instructors within the fire department would be on the same scale as the other firefighters, and salary would be determined by rank and the number of years in service.

Trainers who travel to different cities for the National Fire Academy bid on the classes they will teach. The average pay could range from $2,500 to $3,000, which would cover their expenses and a fee for their time.

The rewards trainers report are more than financial, however. Trainers derive great satisfaction from seeing their students gain confidence while they are learning all the necessary skills. If a department runs smoothly, and each firefighter does an exceptional job, some of the credit goes to the trainer.

Let's Meet...

Glenn Joseph
Trainer

In addition to being a firefighter/ paramedic and a fire safety inspector, Glenn is also a firefighter instructor. Firefighting is his first love and everything else is what he does on the side.

How did you get started as a firefighter?

I was going to school, and during the summers I worked in a hospital emergency room. From there I got into emergency medical services. I became a paramedic 10 or 12 years ago, and then decided to become a firefighter.

In addition to being a firefighter/ paramedic, tell us about your role as trainer.

I teach classes here at the fire department, and at the regional training center. I teach basic and advanced firefighting skills. I usually teach on my days off, but sometimes I teach a class here at my station during my shift.

What's it like in the classroom?

Well, sometimes when I'm teaching at my department, the whole class has to get up and leave when there's a fire.

It's a lot of responsibility. You want to give out the right information. You have to do a lot of research.

It's kind of hard to teach the people you work with. It's like a family; they all know you and all your habits. You have to command respect by knowing your material, and you also have to be able to make the material interesting. Firefighters like action and excitement, and not all the material is as exciting as you would think.

What do you like most about teaching?

It keeps my own skills very fresh and refined. In order to teach a particular subject or skill, I have to know it well. It keeps me on the cutting edge of what's going on.

It also helps me keep firefighters safe. There's strong focus on safety, health, and physical fitness. I'd like to think I'm making the work environment a little safer.

But most of all, I like seeing what happens at the end of a six-week course I'm teaching. I've had new students who have never seen firefighting before and don't know what they're getting into. They don't have good organizational skills; they don't know about working as a team. Then six weeks later, I see them working as a very cohesive team. They communicate with each other and tell each other what they need to get the job done. Teamwork is the most important thing in the fire service.

Is there anything you don't like about teaching?

It does tend to be repetitive. We have to teach some of the same information every year, so we have to think of new ways to present the same material to the same people. It takes a lot of time and preparation.

An Impossible Question

Here's a question Glenn poses to new recruits. How would you answer it?

You are a firefighter and you and your partner are trapped in a burning building with a civilian. The building is just about to collapse. Your partner and the civilian are both injured, but you can carry only one out. Whoever you leave in will definitely die. Which one do you rescue?

This is a dilemma that firefighters face every day. There's no right or wrong answer. If you were the civilian, what would you want the firefighter to do?

What if you were the injured partner? Who would you expect your partner to save?

Firefighters are taught not to leave the building without their partner. But they also take an oath to help and protect civilians, to give up their life for the people they serve.

Could you handle having to make this decision?

Let's Meet...

Captain John Clarke
Training and Safety Officer

John is responsible for all the training that goes on in his department. He is also responsible for the health and safety of the department. He has been with the fire service for more than thirty years, the last six as a training officer.

What are your duties?

I work nine to five. My duties as a training officer are to see that the level of training complies with regulations and guidelines from various organizations. I hire trainers to do that. They could work for our department or be from the fire academy. And I do arrange training provided by the National Fire Academy.

As safety officer, I inspect our stations to make sure they're safe; that there are no extension cords lying around, or open plugs, and that we have fire extinguishers and exit lights that work. I also make sure our equipment and our practices are safe. I'm involved not only in writing the rules, but in their enforcement.

I also investigate any accidents involving our vehicles, and I review all accidents that happen in the city.

What kind of training does a new recruit go through?

He or she gets all the basics of firefighting—fire hydraulics, the use of ladders, water supplies, breathing equipment, patient handling, hose handling, hazardous materials, firefighting tactics, ropes, knots, utility tools such as pry bars and axes, and all the other equipment.

After new recruits have been trained at the fire academy or a community college, they spend a few weeks in orientation to show them our way. We give them background on how everything works here.

What do you like most about your job?

The rewarding side is seeing people move from one level of expertise to another. It's a very rewarding career because there are times you feel you have made a difference and have changed the outcome of a situation.

What do you like least about your job?

Being a training officer can be boring; it's a desk job and there's a lot of paperwork. I worked my way up through the ranks and was a platoon commander for fifteen years. I liked that job a lot. I liked going on the calls and being involved with all the different emergencies.

The more you advance, the more you are removed from the action, and why you became a firefighter in the first place. But you also have to serve where the chief tells you to serve. That's part of the job.

John Clarke's Typical Day

The first thing John does in the morning is to make sure he's not going to have any problems with the classes. Is the instructor there and is he prepared? Does he need any equipment? Is the classroom ready?

Then he checks to make sure there are no scheduling conflicts.

Often, John sits in on classes to see if the instructors are providing the information he expects.

John also has to work on his schedule of classes for the next few months, order equipment, and attend committee meetings. And there are always different projects his boss gives him. Recently, he was working on a vehicle operation handbook that will be put in each vehicle.

After lunch, John helps other people with their projects.

Success Story

These days, it's fairly easy to call for help when there's a fire. Most cities are hooked up to a central dispatch system. Simply picking up the phone and dialing 911 will bring the fire department. Many city street corners and public buildings also have pull-alarm systems that alert a local department to a fire's location; some have voiceboxes, which enable the caller to talk directly with the department.

Modern firefighters can communicate easily with each other, through radios in their trucks and handheld cellular phones. Most modern fire departments pride themselves in having a five-minute-or-less response time to a fire emergency.

But in early times, communication was not that easy. The first to spot a fire would run out to the street using the only tool available then—the human voice. But yelling "fire" didn't always ensure quick action.

Trumpets came into use in the 1800s. They were good tools for directing and amplifying the human voice. Firefighters used trumpets to shout orders to each other or to sound the alarm for a fire. They also had good secondary uses; they became handy clubs to break up fights between rival fire companies battling over water supplies.

Trumpets were made of solid brass, nickel plate, or tole (painted tin). Trumpets given as gifts to retiring chiefs, for example, were made of silver plate or solid silver. Some even had gold plating and were inlaid with semi-precious stones.

Trumpets, along with any antique fire paraphernalia, such as helmets, badges, and leather buckets, are all valuable collector's items.

Find Out More

You and firefighting training

These are the five most important qualities that trainers try to teach their new recruits:

1. **Attitude:** If you really want to do something, you can do much more than you think you can.

2. **Teamwork:** Being able to work as part of a team is the most important skill a fire-fighter can learn.

3. **Creativity:** How to use the skills and knowledge you have to come up with a solution to a problem.

4. **Physical Strength:** Fire-fighters must stay strong and fit, and working out is part of their daily regimen.

5. **Emotional Strength:** Fire-fighters spend a great deal of emotional energy dealing with people in pain.

Find out more about firefighting training

For more information about careers as a trainer write to:

The National Fire Academy
16825 South Seton Avenue
Emittsburg, MD 21727

ADMINISTRATORS

Most firefighters choose their profession because they love the excitement and challenge. They are used to working on a team and would not want to miss out on that part of the job.

But in every profession, there have to be leaders and organizers. Firefighting organizations need good administrators—men and women who have paid their dues rising through the ranks and are fully aware of the needs of the department. Being brave and daring is not enough.

Administrative positions

Although job titles might vary from city to city and state to state, the responsibilities are generally the same.

Starting at the top, here is a list of different administrative positions you would encounter in most fire departments.

Fire Chief

The fire chief is in charge of the entire organization. That organization could be countywide or citywide, with several fire stations located throughout the zone.

The fire chief works with whatever government body is responsible for fire and rescue functions, planning services and seeing that the plans are put into action. It's the chief's duty to manage the organization with its resources, personnel and equipment, to meet those goals the city has established.

The fire chief can be appointed by a government official, but as is more and more common, he or she will have been a career firefighter who has gone through the ranks.

Deputy Chief/Assistant Chief

Some cities have only one deputy chief, who is responsible for all the divisions within the organization. Other cities could have several assistants or deputies, each responsible for a different division.

In the absence of the fire chief, the deputy chief is responsible. He or she will take over the day-to-day command, or will represent the department, attending meetings in the chief's place.

Division Chief/Battalion Chief/ Captain/Commander
Division chiefs command the following departments:

Training—responsible for maintaining continuing education units for both firefighters and EMS personnel.

Resource management division/support services/ purchasing—responsible for every item purchased, all the equipment and supplies. Also responsible for the maintenance of fire/rescue vehicles.

Fire prevention/public education—responsible for fire inspectors and all programs dealing with the public.

EMS—responsible for all the emergency medical care given on different shifts. This division head monitors personnel, vacations and days off, and scheduling, and must ensure that all the vehicles have enough crew members and paramedics.

Operations—responsible for all the firefighting shifts. The duties are similar to those of the EMS division head.

Supervisors—Many departments also have supervisors who report directly to division heads. They might supervise the hour-by-hour activities of a shift and follow the trucks out on calls.

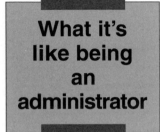

What it's like being an administrator

Being an administrator can be as challenging as being a firefighter. Top administrators have to balance the needs of the community with the money they're given to make the program work. They might have to go to commission meetings and stand in front of public hearings defending their program. Their job is to sell the program and not let someone cut the budget. A lot of jobs depend on how well the top administrator does his job. If a department is mismanaged, a poor level of service is given to the public.

As an administrator, you will no longer work closely as part of a firefighting team. As soon as you are promoted to a supervisory position, you have to deal with leaving your friends behind. You might even be responsible for supervising former coworkers, and that can be awkward.

Getting ahead

It is important for future administrators to develop good writing, speaking, and reading skills. In today's fire service, candidates for promotion take an exam that tests written skills, reading comprehension, and technical knowledge.

Your verbal skills will also be tested in an oral interview, and specific administrative skills will be assessed in role-playing activities. You will be judged on how you make tactical decisions in firefighting situations, how you handle administrative situations, and how you deal with personnel problems.

Ongoing employee evaluations and recommendations from your supervisors will also play a part in whether or not you are promoted.

Many of the specific skills you will need to move up the ladder can be developed on the job. Assist your supervisors with their duties and take business and management courses when they are offered.

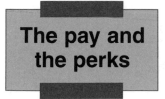

The pay and the perks

Administrative salaries reflect the level of responsibility, but vary from city to city and state to state. Fire chiefs can earn between $85,000 and $100,000 a year, sometimes more.

Vacation and sick time is generally based on the number of years of service. A deputy chief with 17 years on the force will get the same number of days as a firefighter who has put in 17 years.

Let's Meet...

Harry "H.L." Small
Commander of
Emergency Medical Services

Harry oversees three supervisors and 65 paramedics. He started in 1976 as a volunteer firefighter, worked his way through the ranks as a firefighter/ paramedic, and became commander in 1991.

Can you tell us about your duties?

I used to be a paramedic, but my job now is to make sure that all the EMTs and paramedics have everything they need to do their job. I make sure the EMTs and paramedics are properly trained.

I oversee the warehouse operation, ordering supplies and buying equipment. I have to make sure the trucks are properly stocked.

I plan a budget and administer it. I keep records on all personnel and equipment and the maintenance of vehicles.

I deal with conflicts and listen to the problems of my employees. Whatever is wrong, I try to fix it. I also deal with anyone in the general public who calls us with a problem.

There are a lot of meetings to attend and state guidelines to follow, too. Paramedics have to write reports for each call they go on. The supervisors have to make sure they are filed properly, so I have to review all of this paperwork.

Mainly, my job is to support the system that's working and make sure the system continues to work.

Do you enjoy your work?

I really miss working in the field. This job is not as exciting. Periodically, I go out and ride with the team just to have a part in it, but it's not the same. I have to get my satisfaction from watching them do well. If they do well, I feel good. You have to learn to enjoy your success through other people—that's a manager's role.

What advice would you have for someone wanting to follow in your footsteps?

Education is crucial these days. Someone interested in this position should think about earning a college degree—in Emergency Medical Services (EMS) and fire science—because that's becoming more and more important. There aren't many 4-year degree programs now, it's mainly at the 2-year level. In coming years, there will be more and more 4-year programs. It's also a good idea to take some college courses in business.

In fire departments with an EMS division an EMS background is advisable. New leaders will be coming from the paramedic corps, which was uncommon in the past.

And when opportunities for learning new skills present themselves, take advantage of them. Study management, human development, handling conflict, anything related to your work. Seek it out.

A Special Thank You

Harry's team received a panicky call from the family of a woman who was feeling sick and had a history of heart problems. They were worried she was having a heart attack.

   The team responded to the call and got everything under control. Then they got the woman to the hospital, and she came through okay.

   Later, Harry received this letter.

> Dear Sir,
>   Through this letter my wife and I wish to express our heartfelt gratitude for the promptness in answering our emergency call, made on Saturday, July 16th. As residents of this city for the past 25 years, we wish to note with great satisfaction the existence of such a service and the fine team who rendered their help in the nick of time. We take pride in being part of this community and thank you for your proud care and attention.

   Receiving a letter of thanks like this one is what Harry says makes the job worthwhile.

Let's Meet...

Anthony "Tony" Stravino
Deputy Chief

Tony is in charge of EMS and the daily operations divisions. He's had more than twenty years of firefighting experience and has been deputy chief since 1990.

What is your job like?

I have two division chiefs below me; one in charge of training and the resource management division, and the other, head of the fire prevention and fire investigation division. Altogether we have 106 people. They have personal problems, family problems, divorce, whatever, and sometimes they just want to let off steam. That's what I'm here for. I also make discipline, hiring, and firing recommendations to the fire chief.

What are some of the challenges of your work?

You have a lot of different personalities to deal with. We have a lot of people who love the thrill of going to the fires. It's tough to manage these people, because what makes them so good as firefighters also makes them difficult to deal with. You want a highly assertive, highly aggressive person who wants to get into these situations and isn't afraid of anything. However, after the emergency is over and you are back to day-to-day things, that person is used to getting his way, and getting it fast. You spend a lot of time trying to tone them down.

What do you like most about your work?

After you get the normal day-to-day work out of the way, every day is different. I'm involved in every aspect of the organization.

Another advantage is that, as the deputy chief, I can go to any fire or on any call. Because I'm here five days a week, I get to see a lot more than when I was on shift.

I don't usually get suited up, but I do keep the uniform and equipment in my car. The other night I helped out at a church fire, but that's not the norm. Usually when I go, it's to assist the on-duty commander and to make sure the operational end is working right.

When you're on the scene, you can identify any problems in the operation. I can see if our training program is working well, and if not, I can decide where to put more emphasis.

How does someone move into a top administrative position?

You have to develop skills through your work. When I became deputy chief, I came up from the position of division chief of training and resource management. When the person who was deputy at the time was on vacation, I worked for him, getting a feel for what he was doing over the years. I learned what skills were required. If there are some tasks or skills you don't feel sure about, you can study them.

Little League, Firefighting, and Mom

Tony played Little League baseball and football, and during almost every game, the coaches would have to leave when their pagers went off. They were all volunteer firefighters.

"A lot of my friends' dads were volunteers, too," Tony explains, "and we went on picnics and to parties and, then they'd be called off again.

"I was in my junior year of college and I took the firefighting exam just for practice. My plan was to finish college first and then try again. But I passed and I scored very well.

"I was also lucky because they had some openings right away. I was the first kid in my family to work toward a four-year degree and my mother really wanted me to finish college. I took the job but I promised her I would finish."

After two years of paramedic school, Tony took six months off and finished his bachelor's degree in business administration. Currently he's working on a master's in public administration, and as Tony admits, "My mother is very happy."

Success Story

Ben Franklin and the Bucket Brigade

In 1736 in Philadelphia, Benjamin Franklin organized the first permanent fire company.

Before then, city-dwellers had only volunteer bucket brigades to protect them. As early as 1686, most houses in New York City were required to have a bucket hanging near the front door. When they heard the cry of "fire," residents would toss out their buckets to firemen and other citizens, who would pick them up and join the bucket brigade.

The bucket brigade consisted of two lines: the first line would pass filled buckets from the water supply (usually a cistern, a tank that caught and stored rainwater) to the fire; the second line passed the empty buckets back for refilling.

Early fire buckets were made of leather and had their owner's name or initials painted in oil on them. Some were decorated with elaborate coats-of-arms or oil portraits. These decorations were required so owners could claim their buckets after a fire.

Today, these leather buckets are collectors' items and are very valuable.

Find Out More

To determine who will be promoted to administrative positions, candidates are put through a series of tests.

One test involves role-playing. Here's the situation. Can you see a solution?

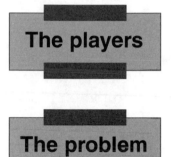

The players

A disgruntled, unhappy firefighter.

The firefighter's supervisor.

You, the deputy chief.

The problem

The supervisor has just ordered the firefighter to mop the floor. The firefighter has refused. Why? The supervisor, who is much younger than the firefighter, has just been promoted to the position—a position the firefighter wanted.

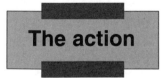

The action

The firefighter says to his new supervisor: "I'm a lot older than you, I've been here a lot longer, but they picked you, and I'm not going to listen to you."

The supervisor says: "You have to do what I tell you to do."

He still refuses so they go to see you—the deputy chief.

Your goal is to get the two people involved to see eye to eye. What steps would you take?

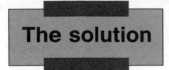

The solution

Step 1. Talk to the supervisor privately. You have to calm him down. He's new and he's upset. He gave an order. Back him up but suggest that the way he presented the order could possibly have been done differently.

Step 2. Talk with the firefighter privately. He studied for the promotion but he didn't get it. Offer the department's assistance in helping him to improve for the next promotion period. Then you ask him to put himself in his supervisor's shoes. He's going to be a supervisor soon, and how would he feel if a firefighter refused to obey one of his orders?

Step 3. Everyone is calmer and ready to talk. You bring both players into your office together. They can each see the other's position now. They both apologize and go back to work.

Step 4. Congratulations! You have passed, and you are now the new deputy chief.

Find out more about firefighting administration

For more information about careers as a firefighting administrator, contact:

International Association of Fire
    Chiefs
4025 Fair Ridge Drive
Fairfax, VA 22033–2868

INDEX

VGM CAREER BOOKS

CAREER DIRECTORIES
Careers Encyclopedia
Dictionary of Occupational
  Titles
Occupational Outlook
  Handbook

CAREERS FOR
Animal Lovers
Bookworms
Computer Buffs
Crafty People
Culture Lovers
Environmental Types
Film Buffs
Foreign Language Aficionados
Good Samaritans
Gourmets
History Buffs
Kids at Heart
Nature Lovers
Night Owls
Number Crunchers
Plant Lovers
Shutterbugs
Sports Nuts
Travel Buffs

CAREERS IN
Accounting; Advertising;
Business; Child Care;
Communications; Computers;
Education; Engineering;
the Environment; Finance;
Government; Health Care;
High Tech; Journalism; Law;
Marketing; Medicine;
Science; Social &
Rehabilitation Services

CAREER PLANNING
Admissions Guide to Selective
  Business Schools
Beating Job Burnout
Beginning Entrepreneur
Career Planning &
  Development for College
  Students & Recent Graduates
Career Change

Careers Checklists
Cover Letters They Don't
  Forget
Executive Job Search Strategies
Guide to Basic Cover Letter
  Writing
Guide to Basic Resume Writing
Guide to Temporary
  Employment
Job Interviews Made Easy
Joyce Lain Kennedy's Career
  Book
Out of Uniform
Resumes Made Easy
Slam Dunk Resumes
Successful Interviewing for
  College Seniors
Time for a Change

CAREER PORTRAITS
Animals	Nursing
Cars	Sports
Computers	Teaching
Music	Travel

GREAT JOBS FOR
Communications Majors
English Majors
Foreign Language Majors
History Majors
Psychology Majors

HOW TO
Approach an Advertising
  Agency and Walk Away with
  the Job You Want
Bounce Back Quickly After
  Losing Your Job
Choose the Right Career
Find Your New Career Upon
  Retirement
Get & Keep Your First Job
Get Hired Today
Get into the Right Business
  School
Get into the Right Law School
Get People to Do Things Your
  Way
Have a Winning Job Interview

Hit the Ground Running in
  Your New Job
Improve Your Study Skills
Jump Start a Stalled Career
Land a Better Job
Launch Your Career in TV
  News
Make the Right Career Moves
Market Your College Degree
Move from College into a
  Secure Job
Negotiate the Raise You
  Deserve
Prepare a Curriculum Vitae
Prepare for College
Run Your Own Home Business
Succeed in College
Succeed in High School
Write a Winning Resume
Write Successful Cover Letters
Write Term Papers & Reports
Write Your College Application
  Essay

OPPORTUNITIES IN
This extensive series provides
detailed information on nearly
150 individual career fields.

RESUMES FOR
Advertising Careers
Banking and Financial Careers
Business Management Careers
College Students &
  Recent Graduates
Communications Careers
Education Careers
Engineering Careers
Environmental Careers
50 + Job Hunters
Health and Medical Careers
High School Graduates
High Tech Careers
Law Careers
Midcareer Job Changes
Sales and Marketing Careers
Scientific and Technical Careers
Social Service Careers
The First-Time Job Hunter

 VGM Career Horizons
a division of *NTC Publishing Group*
4255 West Touhy Avenue
Lincolnwood, Illinois 60646–1975